Will Rogers

Will Rogers

Quotable Cowboy

by Cathereen L. Bennett

RP **Runestone Press • Minneapolis**

RUNESTONE PRESS • RΠ▸ΓRↂ

rune (rōōn) *n* **1 a :** one of the earliest written alphabets used in northern Europe, dating back to A.D. 200; **b :** an alphabet character believed to have magic powers; **c :** a charm; **d :** an Old Norse or Finnish poem. **2 :** a poem or incantation of mysterious significance, often carved in stone.

Thanks to Joseph Carter, Patricia Lowe, and Greg Malak of the Will Rogers Memorial and Birthplace in Claremore, Oklahoma, for their help with this project.

Will Rogers: Quotable Cowboy is a fully revised and updated edition of *Will Rogers: The Cowboy Who Walked with Kings,* a title previously published by Lerner Publications Company. The text is completely reset in 11/13 New Baskerville, and new photographs and captions have been added.

The sources for quotes in the margins are listed on p. 94.

Library of Congress Cataloging-in-Publication Data
  Bennett, Cathereen L.
    Will Rogers : quotable cowboy / Cathereen L. Bennett.
      p. cm.
    Includes index.
    ISBN 0–8225–3155–0 (lib. bdg.)
    1. Rogers, Will, 1879–1935—Juvenile literature. 2. Entertainers—United States—Biography—Juvenile literature. 3. Humorists, American—Biography—Juvenile literature. I. Title.
PN2287.R74B39 1995
792.7'028'092—dc20   95–10259
  [B]   CIP
                                                                   AC

Manufactured in the United States of America
1 2 3 4 5 6 – JR – 00 99 98 97 96 95

482434

Contents

Will Rogers . . . is what Americans think other Americans are like.

—*The New York Sun,* April 5, 1935

As a young boy, Will Rogers dreamed of being a cowboy.

1 The Making of a Cowboy

Throughout his life, Will Rogers was happiest twirling a rope while riding a quick-moving horse. He began riding not long after he started walking, and he had his own horse at the age of five. Nearly every day, he practiced twirling his rope, or lariat, and catching objects with the loop—the skills Will thought all cowboys needed to have. As a young boy, Will learned all the well-known tricks and even invented many of his own. A keen interest in roping and riding came naturally to him, as it did to many children who grew up on the prairies of the midwestern United States.

Will was born on November 4, 1879, on his father's cattle ranch near Oologah, Indian Territory, which later became part of Oklahoma. His parents named him William Penn Adair Rogers. Both his mother, Mary, and his father, Clem, were part Cherokee. Clem was a senator in the Cherokee Nation (the government of the Cherokee), and Will took pride in his Indian heritage.

“*Live your life so that whenever you lose, you are ahead.***”**

Will grew up on his family's ranch in Oologah, Indian Territory (now part of Oklahoma). To help him learn about ranching, Will's father gave him a small herd of calves to raise.

Will's mother, who was gentle and fun loving, hoped that he would become a Methodist minister. His father, a gruff and reserved man, just wanted him to "amount to something." But as Will grew up, Clem often shook his head, angry and puzzled at his son's carefree ways. The youngest of five children, Willie, as his family called him, often got into mischief. One day, for example, young Willie decided that the family hunting dogs would look better with spots, so he covered the animals with patches of green paint.

Will started his education at the age of seven in a one-room schoolhouse. From the beginning,

Will's parents, Mary (right) and Clem (below), were opposite in many ways. Mary enjoyed music and dancing, thought an education was important, and was very religious. Clem was a strong believer in hard work and strict discipline.

Young Will shows off his new bicycle. Bicycling became a national craze in the 1890s, when the first bicycles with air-filled rubber tires and adjustable handlebars were introduced.

the restless boy found it difficult to concentrate on his ABC's. It wasn't that Will lacked intelligence. He was just bored. He preferred activity to study, and he hated being confined indoors with good sunshine going to waste. Will thought that roping fence posts was more exciting than history, and swapping ponies was much more fun than math.

Will was not an industrious boy. When he should have been doing chores, he could usually be found in a shady place playing with his rope. He spent most of his after-school time racing his pony with his friends. His parents thought Will should spend more time doing his homework, but Will saw himself as a cowboy in the making.

Will's teacher worried about his lack of interest in school and talked to the boy's parents about it. His father became exasperated with the poor quality of Will's schoolwork. Thinking that Will might settle down to his studies if he was away from his horse and his fun-loving friends, Clem sent his son to a boarding school in Muskogee, Oklahoma.

Before Will left, Mary talked earnestly to her son about the importance of education, trying to instill in the youth a desire for book learning. She realized that Will had long ago decided that what a cowboy needed to know could not be found between the covers of a book. But, for his mother's sake, Will promised to try to do well at his new school.

Will did try. He was good natured and not deliberately mischievous. He made friends easily and soon became a favorite with the other

"I got just as far as McGuffey's Fourth Reader *when the teacher wouldn't seem to be running the school right, and rather than have the school stop, I would generally leave."*

At Kemper Military Academy in Missouri, Will wore a uniform and learned military drills.

students. They enjoyed his stories of ranch life and greatly admired his roping skill.

In the spring of 1890, when Will was ten years old, his mother died of typhoid fever. Will was deeply saddened by her death. All his life, he never forgot her kindness and understanding.

The next fall, he returned to boarding school, where his roping skill proved to be his undoing. One afternoon Will was practicing with his loop in what he thought was a safely deserted spot by the side of a building. Unfortunately one of the teachers was out for a leisurely after-dinner stroll. As the teacher calmly rounded a corner of the building, Will caught and threw him in the dust like a range cow. Will immediately helped the shaken man to his feet, freed him of the rope, and attempted to explain and apologize. The red-faced teacher refused the boy's stammered explanation and had him dismissed from school.

Will returned to the family ranch and pleaded with his father to let him stay home. Clem ignored Will's pleas and sent him to another boarding school. As in every school he attended, Will was extremely popular. He could turn any situation into a joke, and he enjoyed entertaining his friends. Although he had a quick mind and a good memory, Will could never take school very seriously. There was too much else to do.

When Will was about sixteen, his father sent him to a military school in Missouri, hoping that the strict discipline imposed on the cadets would tame him. Will traded his chaps and boots for a snug-fitting, high-collared cadet's uniform. At first he enjoyed the military academy. He liked to shine his rifle and parade around the school

During his two years at Kemper, Will (front row, second from right) *played on the school's football team.*

grounds. But, after a few weeks, the strict routine began to smother his lighthearted personality. He unsuccessfully tried to fit his leisurely walk to the smart military step required of him. Worst of all, Will was forbidden to practice with his beloved rope. He felt the loss keenly and sighed frequently over his books. Will spent two years at the academy before his spirit rebelled completely. He slipped away one dark night, deciding to "quit the entire school business for life."

Will sits atop Comanche, his favorite horse.

2 A Taste of Freedom

Not wanting to face his father and determined to prove himself, Will made his way southward from Missouri to Texas, where his ability with horse and rope won him a job on a ranch near the town of Higgins. Although only eighteen, the ex-schoolboy pulled his weight when the ranch hands drove a herd of cattle northward to Kansas for slaughtering. Despite his youth, he was shown no favors and asked for none. This was the life he had always wanted, and, in Will's opinion, the tiresome bawling of the cattle and the bone-weary ache in his body were small prices to pay.

Will was on the trail from sunup to sundown. And he had to take his turn at night watch. But he reveled in his freedom and cheerfully rode day after day in the choking cloud of dust raised by the moving herd. At night he slept under the stars, using his saddle as a pillow. Each morning he rose happily to eat beans and sip coffee.

When Will received his wages in Kansas, he again headed south, this time to Amarillo, Texas.

" . . . Every man has wanted to be a cowboy. Why play Wall Street and die young when you can play cowboy and never die? "

During the late 1800s, ranchers kept hundreds of cattle on the vast open range of the western United States. Will, who worked on a ranch and drove cattle to market, found cowboy life exciting but tough.

Like Will, this sprawling town—the railway hub of northern Texas—was young but had grown up fast. Will quickly spent his money and wandered around Amarillo for three days before talking his way into a job as a horse wrangler. He took care of the horses as his group moved to Panhandle, Texas, then to Woodward, Oklahoma, where Will helped round up the newborn calves for branding.

After a hard day driving cattle, cowboys enjoyed gathering around the chuckwagon to eat and swap stories.

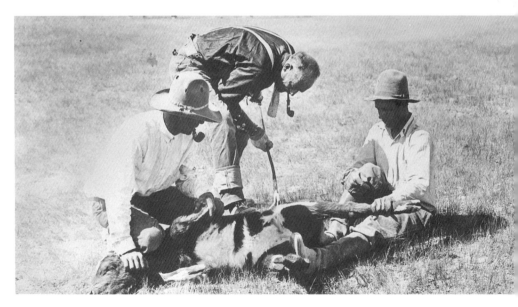

Every spring and fall, cowboys rounded up the herd to brand newborn calves. Each calf was marked with a symbol that identified its owner.

In his early twenties, Will started courting Betty Blake, who shared his love of music and dancing. Betty, who lived in Rogers, Arkansas, worked as a clerk for the railroad and as a typesetter for a local newspaper.

After a spring and a summer as a cowboy, Will headed home. When he arrived in Oologah, he found that his father had surprising plans for the future. Clem had moved from the ranch into the nearby town of Claremore, and he wanted to turn the ranch over to Will. Clem was a well-to-do man who had become very influential in Indian Territory. He was working to obtain statehood for the territory as Oklahoma. With Will to run the ranch, Clem could devote his time to this task and also to the bank he had opened in Claremore.

Will liked the adventurous and carefree life of a cowboy. Ranch owning—and the responsibilities that went with it—was another story. The first thing he did with his new authority was to arrange for the building of a wooden dance platform. During his travels, Will had become an excellent dancer and had won many prizes. Cowboys and fiddlers drifted on and off the ranch as word spread that Will was back home and holding "open house."

During Will's absence, a new arrival had brightened the sleepy cow town of Oologah. Betty Blake had come from Arkansas to see her sister, and Will lost his heart the first time he saw the pretty visitor walking down Oologah's dusty wooden sidewalk.

Will courted Betty earnestly. He took her riding in an open buggy, showing her the places he loved—the stream where he caught his first fish, the huge shade tree under which he had practiced his roping as a small boy, and the now-abandoned little schoolhouse he had attended. But Betty had to return home at Christmastime.

Betty (third from bottom) *and her six sisters pose for a photograph. Betty also had two brothers.*

During the next year or so, Will and Betty wrote to one another. Soon, however, their long-distance romance began to fade.

By the fall of 1900, Will was itching to move on. He spent as much time off the ranch as he did on it. Leaving the ranch in the care of hired hands, Will traveled as far east as New York and as far west as California. There, after tending a trainload of cattle, Will and his bunkmate, a fellow cowboy, blew out the gaslight in their hotel room without turning off the gas. All night long, the poisonous substance seeped into the room. In the morning, both cowboys were unconscious and close to death. After many hours, doctors revived the pair, but they were still very weak. Will returned to Oklahoma to get well.

After Will had recovered, he headed to Missouri to try his luck in steer-roping contests. During a cattle drive, cowboys rode at a gallop to rope steers that had strayed too far from the herd. Steer roping required a lot of strength and coordination. In competitions a steer was sent running into an arena, where the cowboy waited on horseback. The roper chased the steer, threw a loop over the animal's horns, and then rode in the other direction with the end of the rope secured to the saddle. As the cowboy rode away, the loop tightened, pulling the steer to the ground. The roper then got off the horse, ran to the steer, and tied all four of its legs together. The contestant who accomplished this difficult variety of tasks in the least amount of time won the competition.

At one steer-roping contest, Will met Colonel Zach Mulhall, who gave him his first taste of show

> **"There ought to be a law against anybody going to Europe till they had seen the things we have in this country."**

During his travels, Will and a friend stopped at Niagara Falls, which borders the state of New York and the Canadian province of Ontario.

business. Later Will said that it ruined him for life as far as actual employment was concerned. Colonel Mulhall, whom Will called simply "the Colonel," saw the young cowboy at a steer-roping contest in St. Louis, Missouri. The Colonel worked for a railroad company in California but spent his free time staging riding and roping contests.

During his stay in Missouri, the Colonel was putting together a "cowboy band." He hired real musicians and dressed them in chaps, boots, spurs, and broad-brimmed hats. Then he looked around for some honest-to-goodness cowboys who knew horses and roping. Will and fellow cowboy Jim O'Donnell signed up. Will was given a trombone that he couldn't play a note on. He just held it to his lips.

The band went on tour in the midwestern United States, appearing at state fairs. When a sizable crowd had gathered, Colonel Mulhall would challenge the onlookers to produce anyone who could beat his boys at steer roping. Deceived by the talent of the musicians and the newness of their cowboy outfits, members of the crowd would eagerly meet the challenge and place their bets. Then Will and Jim would saddle up and prove their skill.

Will enjoyed his work with the cowboy band. The pay wasn't regular, but the company was good. At the state fair in San Antonio, Texas, he met a tall cowboy named Tom Mix. Tom and Will soon became friends. Although Tom was a year younger than Will, he had traveled more. Tom had been to China and also had fought in Cuba with Teddy Roosevelt (who was later elected pres-

"Everybody is ignorant, only on different subjects."

Will, pictured here at age twenty, was always looking for adventure.

ident of the United States) and the famous Rough Riders in the Spanish-American War. Both Will and Tom agreed that they'd been bitten by the show-business bug. Tom Mix eventually became one of the country's most famous movie cowboys.

Will's conversations with Tom had given him a new curiosity. The Oklahoma cowboy began to yearn for faraway places. So he decided to pack his bags and go looking for adventure.

Wearing a red velvet costume, Will entertains a crowd in Australia during an early performing tour. Will's rope tricks brought a taste of the American Wild West to faraway locations, such as South Africa, Australia, and New Zealand.

26

3 Adventures Abroad

Will had heard a lot about Argentina, a cattle-raising country in South America. There the cattle fed on native grasses in vast fields and weren't penned in by barbed wire. Will longed to work in Argentina's wide-open spaces. So, with his pockets full of money he had earned by selling his cattle, he decided to take a look.

By this time, Will's sister May and her husband, Frank Stine, were living on the ranch, so Will felt free to roam. In early 1902, he teamed up with another footloose cowhand named Dick Parris. Together they went to New Orleans, Louisiana, a port from which they thought they could sail to South America.

The charming southern city at the mouth of the Mississippi River provided many delights. New Orleans's shops were filled with costly European imports, and the city's architecture was varied and elaborate. The chants of food vendors pierced the air as they sold the day's catch of fish in stalls along the crowded, cobblestone streets.

"I can't tell you where to write for I don't know where I will be."

In the early 1900s, huge steamships carried passengers across the world's oceans. In New York, Will and his friend Dick Parris boarded a ship bound for Great Britain.

Although New Orleans had much to offer, it proved a disappointment to Will and Dick. The harbor was busy with the traffic of many boats, but not one vessel traveled to South America. Disappointed but determined, the adventurers made their way north to New York, only to learn that they had missed the yearly ship to Buenos Aires, the capital of Argentina. Because their hearts were set on a sea voyage, the two friends decided to book passage to Britain and to make their way from there to South America.

Will had never traveled by boat. A saddle horse had always been his chief means of locomotion. Even before the ship had cleared New York's harbor, Will felt a slight twinge. He lasted on deck just long enough to envy the Statue of Liberty its solid mooring. The Oklahoma cowboy spent the entire trip across the North Atlantic Ocean groaning and tossing in his bunk, miserably seasick. Will was certain that the heaving ship was more lively than any bucking bronco. He landed in Britain determined to stay "until some enterprising party built a bridge back home."

Will and Dick were greatly impressed with London, Britain's capital, and toured the city tirelessly. Preparations were being made for the coronation of a new king, Edward VII. Will liked the bright-colored uniforms and tall fur hats of the guards at the king's palace, and he was amused by the rapid speech of the British. One time Will told a man that he would gladly pay him overtime if he would just talk slower.

Will's memory of his agonizing boat trip dimmed during the passing weeks. Still anxious to see Argentina, he and Dick boarded a boat for Brazil, another South American country. Will had the same unpleasant experience on this voyage. Unable to eat, weak and dizzy, he spent most of the trip below deck, while Dick strolled topside, thoroughly enjoying the voyage and eagerly answering the dinner gong. Twenty-three days later, the ship docked, and Will, his suffering over, happily set foot on dry land.

After the two young men had traveled from Brazil to Argentina, their money was nearly gone. Dick developed a serious case of homesickness,

"I always wondered why the British drink so much tea. Now I know because I've tasted their coffee."

but between them, the friends had only enough money to pay for one fare home. Will let Dick take the money to return and remained behind to work on cattle drives for the equivalent of about $7.50 a month.

Will traveled the length and breadth of Argentina's cattle country for five months, never staying long in one place and not making much money. Argentines speak Spanish, and Will's only language was the ungrammatical English of a rough cowhand. But his obvious friendliness and good humor overcame the language barrier.

Will was itching to display his roping technique to the gauchos (Argentine cowboys) until he witnessed their amazing skill with the bola. A bola is a rawhide sling four to six feet in length, weighted at the ends with stones or iron balls. Gauchos throw their bolas with remarkable accuracy and can stop a running steer instantly by entangling the bola in the animal's legs. Will later insisted that the gauchos could throw a bola as far as he could shoot a Winchester rifle.

While in Argentina, Will heard tales of the Boer War, a conflict in South Africa between the British and the Boers (Dutch-descended landowners in South Africa.) Still without funds, he decided to try his luck on another continent. He didn't welcome the thought of the boat trip but swallowed his reluctance and went to the harbor to look for work. A steamer bound for Africa was taking on a load of mules. The gauchos were having difficulty roping and loading the animals. Will could not make himself understood when he asked the foreman for work, so when he spotted a gaucho in trouble with a particularly feisty

"What's the matter with the world? There ain't nothing but one word wrong with every one of us, and that's selfishness."

mule, he uncoiled his lariat and caught the rearing animal. He immediately had a job roping mules for twenty-five cents apiece.

A British rancher named Piccione owned the steamer with the lively cargo, and he hired Will to help tend the animals on the crossing. Will fared a little better on this trip. A few cows and calves accompanied the mules, and caring for the animals kept Will so busy that he didn't have time to be seasick. Much to his surprise, Will discovered that he still had his appetite. Not getting enough food to satisfy it, he began milking the cows at night. Then he traded the milk to the ship's cook for food. The cook was delighted to get fresh milk at sea and kept Will well fed during the month-long crossing.

When Will reached South Africa in September 1902, he had no trouble finding employment. He went to work on Piccione's ranch, where his job included caring for the horses and helping the veterinarian and the blacksmith. About two months later, Will quit and took another job transporting mules to Ladysmith, South Africa.

In Ladysmith Will was overjoyed to discover a Wild West circus. It was like finding a piece of home in a foreign land. The owner, Texas Jack, hired Will on the spot as part of his traveling show. Besides performing rope tricks and riding broncos, Will wore a fancy costume and performed a song-and-dance act. He wanted his audience to know that he had authentic Indian roots, so during the tour he billed himself as "The Cherokee Kid."

After a year in the show, Will considered himself a veteran and wanted to join an even bigger

"Geography don't change human nature. If you are right, people are for you whether it's in Africa or Siberia."

circus. After Texas Jack gave Will a letter of introduction, the restless cowboy shook the dust of South Africa off his boots and sailed for Australia.

Texas Jack's letter got Will a job with the Wirth Brothers Circus in Sydney, Australia. This time, Will limited his act to riding and roping. He soon was a big hit with circus fans. The Australians were great horse lovers, and they recognized and appreciated Will's skill and daring. One afternoon when the circus was not performing, Will entered a horse race meet and tried a new trick. Urging his horse to a full gallop, he hooked his

In South Africa, Texas Jack (right) *hired Will to perform rope tricks in his Wild West Circus. Calling himself "The Cherokee Kid," Will became a headline act.*

toes around the saddle horn and flung his body backward. With the galloping hooves just inches from his head, Will twisted his head and snatched three handkerchiefs from the ground with his teeth. The crowd yelled its delight.

Australia's governor general, a high-ranking official, was in the stands watching the performance. He sent someone over to ask Will to repeat the trick. "Tell him I'll do it again for $150," Will said. The governor general's man was shocked at this demand, but Will could not see that he owed the official any special favors. His face split with the wide, easy grin that was to become so famous, and he drawled, "You tell the governor general if he'll do it cheaper, I'll loan him my horse and handkerchiefs."

After touring Australia, Will and the circus went to New Zealand, an island nation southeast of Australia. When that tour was over, Will took a boat to San Francisco, California, and then a freight train to Oklahoma. The year was 1904, and Will was back home.

Texas Jack's Wild West Circus included a cowboy band, trick riders, clowns, and ropers. Will, on horseback, is pictured in the center under the number eight.

When Will returned to the United States, Colonel Zach Mulhall (right, holding hat and post) *paid Will* (top center, in circle) *to appear in a Wild West show at the 1904 World's Fair in St. Louis.*

4 A New Home

Once again in familiar territory, Will decided to take a rest after his long journey. The young cowboy had traveled around the world in just over two years and had covered more than 50,000 miles. Home looked mighty good to Will—the faces were friendly and the meals were regular. Best of all, there was no heaving ocean to turn his stomach.

Will had learned many things during his travels, especially about himself. The fun-loving cowboy from Oologah had left the United States caring more about riding and roping than anything else. He returned feeling much the same—with one change. Will had discovered that it was a lot more fun to "punch cows" in front of an audience than on a dusty trail, and besides it paid better.

The townspeople of Claremore, Oklahoma, had become accustomed to the abrupt arrivals and departures of their favorite cowboy, so Will's homecoming did not surprise them. They greeted

You can roam all over the world, but after all, it's what the people at home think of you that really counts.

*Will and Comanche
(facing page)
entertained some of the
twenty million
Americans who
attended the World's
Fair (above).*

him warmly, but Will didn't stay long. He received word that his old friend Colonel Mulhall was getting together a Wild West show. Will said a hasty good-bye to his friends and took a train north to Missouri to join the Colonel in his new venture. The show played at the World's Fair in St. Louis in 1904.

At the fair, Will also had the opportunity to renew his friendship with Betty Blake, whom he hadn't seen in more than four years. While touring the fairgrounds, Betty overheard someone talking about Will's performance in the show. She sent him a note, and Will immediately responded. They met briefly, only long enough for Will to find out that she had not married.

The couple began to write to one another again, and Will made it clear that he wanted to marry her. Betty really liked Will, but she didn't approve of his career and insisted that they just be friends. So they continued to write letters.

When the fair in St. Louis closed, Will left the Colonel's show to try his luck on the stage. He picked Chicago, Illinois, as the place to make his debut in vaudeville, a live stage show that featured a variety of acts. Vaudeville theaters were springing up all over the country, especially in larger cities, to feature this new kind of entertainment. But this type of show wasn't new to Will. The main difference between vaudeville and Texas Jack's Wild West Circus in South Africa was that the actors performed on a wooden stage in front of footlights instead of on the dusty, uneven ground of an arena.

At first Will had no luck getting a job. No one seemed interested in hiring an unknown personality who did rope tricks. Will finally found work by accident. He was buying a ticket at the box office of a Chicago theater when he heard the manager talking on the telephone about needing an act. The desperate theater manager hired Will without an audition. Will dashed to his hotel to get his ropes and was on stage in ten minutes.

The manager kept Will on for the rest of the week. During one performance, a trick dog got loose backstage and dashed across the footlights in front of Will. The cowboy threw his rope quick as lightning and lassoed the unsuspecting dog. The audience loved it.

Will left Chicago after the week was over and returned to his family's ranch. He staked out a

"If you have ever been an actor . . . why it just about ruins you for any useful employment for the rest of your life."

38

In 1905 Colonel Mulhall hired Will and other members of the Wild West Show to perform at Madison Square Garden in New York City.

piece of bare, hard-packed ground the same size as a stage and began training Teddy, a pony he had bought from the Colonel's wife, to work in that limited area. Will decided that if what people really liked was seeing him catch something with his rope, he would be happy to oblige them.

After working for weeks in the small arena, Will left the ranch and agreed to join Colonel Mulhall once more. The Colonel was on his way to New York's Madison Square Garden. Mulhall's Wild West Show had made it to the top of the ladder. Only the best shows appeared at the Garden, and The Colonel knew that Will was the best roper anywhere around.

In the finale of a New York vaudeville show, Will lassoes the cast.

During one of the evening shows at the Garden, a steer used in a roping act got loose from the riders, jumped the arena fence, and ran up into the audience. One thousand pounds of wild steer rampaging through a tightly packed crowd is a fearsome sight. The terrified spectators screamed helplessly as the animal, who was as frightened as they were, plunged into the audience. Will didn't hesitate. He ran up the aisle to head off the steer and threw his rope. He then pulled the steer down into the arena, where other cowboys brought the animal under control.

The next morning, the newspapers published detailed accounts of the quick-thinking cowboy's courageous actions. Will Rogers was front-page news. The shy cowboy was embarrassed to learn that he was a hero. As far as he was concerned, it was just another piece of roping. Will scratched his head and grinned, figuring that these New Yorkers were just a little bit crazy. The newspaper stories did give Will an idea, though. He decided that when the show left town he would stay in New York, performing his roping act on his own.

Solo acts were rare in vaudeville. In fact, they were practically unheard of. But Will kept trying, faithfully making the rounds of the theaters. Disappointed but never discouraged, he wore his boot soles thin walking the sidewalks. Will's fierce determination finally won over one theater manager's skepticism, and he hired Will to do a supper show. These acts were considered

"You see, the subtle thing about a joke is to make it look like it was not a joke."

Will threw two loops at once to rope his horse Teddy and a rider. This popular trick amazed vaudeville audiences.

A dapper Will poses for a vaudeville publicity shot.

unimportant because they played between six and eight o'clock in the evening, when most people were at home eating dinner. Even though Will was playing for only a small and scattered audience, he was content.

In the first few years of his vaudeville career, Will continued to work with his horse Teddy. Small and quick with a calm disposition, the horse was not bothered by the confinement of the theater, the bright footlights, or the backstage confusion. Will covered Teddy's hooves with felt-bottomed galoshes so that the horse would not slip on the smooth waxed boards of the stage.

To display his roping techniques, Will also hired a rider for Teddy. Will had developed a trick of throwing two ropes, one with his left hand and the other with his right. He caught the horse with one loop and the rider with the other. Although the theater audiences enjoyed Will's roping skill, he wasn't much of a hit. It didn't take the cowboy long to realize that audiences enjoyed comedians the most.

For years Will had been amusing his friends with his dry humor, but he dreaded trying to talk to the sea of unknown faces that made up a theater audience. While on stage, Will often made wisecracks to other performers and to offstage workers. The performers saw the value of his lively wit and persuaded him to use his wry humor to introduce the tricks in his act.

Little by little, Will started talking on stage, and he was pleased with the way audiences responded to his remarks. His popularity grew. The restless, rope-throwing cowboy from Oologah had launched his career.

When he took his vaudeville act on the road, Will was the main attraction.

On their honeymoon, Will and Betty visited Niagara Falls.

44

5 "Kinder Nervous"

Success didn't change Will as it has changed many people. He never forgot his cowboy friends or lost his restless spirit. And he never tired of traveling. In 1906 Will again went to Europe. On this trip, he was a performer, not a wandering, footloose cowboy, as he had been before. He played successfully in many countries, but he had one bad experience in Germany. When he roped a firefighter standing offstage, the audience was offended, not amused. Will said that the German people had cultivated everything except a sense of humor.

When Will returned to the United States and became a star attraction in New York earning good money, he began to think of Betty. He wrote to her again and again, often directly proposing marriage. Betty still refused, believing that a life of touring with Will's act just wasn't for her. But Will didn't give up. He continued to send her letters and visited her several times. During one of those visits, Betty finally said yes.

"You got to sorter give and take in this old world. We can get mighty rich, but if we haven't got any friends, we will find we are poorer than anybody."

The Rogers children each took their first riding lesson on their second birthday. Here (from left to right), Bill, Jimmy, Will, and Mary take a ride near their home on Long Island, New York.

Betty and Will were married in 1908 at Betty's home in Rogers, Arkansas, and then the couple went to New York. Betty became Will's partner and business manager, as well as the mother of their four children—Bill, Mary, Jimmy, and Freddie. Will declared, "She's the luckiest thing that ever happened to me." He considered roping Betty the star performance of his life.

Will became even more successful in the years after his marriage. The audiences enjoyed his stories and wisecracks so much that Will began to appear on stage without his horse. He just twirled his rope and talked. In 1912 he appeared at the Victoria, one of New York's largest theaters.

The Rogers's third child, Jimmy, was born in the summer of 1915. That summer was also memorable because it marked the arrival of Dopey, a small, black pony that Will called "the greatest pony for grownups or children anyone ever saw." Dopey became part of the family. He was even allowed in the house, where he walked up and down the stairs.

By family tradition, the Rogers children had their first riding lesson on their second birthday.

Will twirls loops around Jimmy (left) and Mary, while Bill shows off his own roping skill.

They practically grew up on horseback. When Jimmy was two, Will described him as the youngest cowboy in the world. "If you want to start a civil war," Will once said, "just try to take him off that pony. He eats there."

In the meantime, Will had joined the *Ziegfeld Follies*. Florenz Ziegfeld was one of vaudeville's greatest producers. He filled his shows with beautiful women, gorgeous costumes, and elaborate stage sets. Only the best acts played in the Follies. Each evening the rumpled, soft-spoken cowboy entertained sophisticated audiences with his wisecracking humor.

People traveled miles to see the *Follies*, and many came back two and three times to hear Will. Knowing that he was often playing to repeat audiences, Will began worrying that his jokes would get too familiar. As a result, instead of putting together a set routine, as most comedians did, he talked about something different every night.

When he was looking for new topics for his act, Betty suggested that Will talk about what he read in the newspapers. He was in the habit of reading several papers each morning, and he sometimes commented to her on what the politicians were doing. As usual most of Will's remarks were humorous.

Betty's idea took hold, and Will had a never-ending supply of fresh material. He thought that the U.S. Congress, for example, was funnier than anything anyone could make up. He liked to poke fun at the actions of important people, but Will never kidded anyone publicly unless he considered that person able to take the joke.

"Politicians can do more funny things naturally than I can think of to do purposely."

Florenz Ziegfeld (right) *staged the* Ziegfeld Follies, *a show that featured glamorous costumes and scenery. Will, who joined the* Follies *in 1916, sometimes acted out skits. Here* (from left to right), *comics W.C. Fields, Will, Eddie Cantor, and Harry Kelly pretend to compete for Lillian Lorraine's attention.*

Will's wide, sheepish grin made this picture his most famous publicity photo for the **Follies.**

One night in Baltimore, Maryland, just before Will went on stage, he learned that President Woodrow Wilson was in the audience. At this time, the United States was clashing with Mexico, where a rebel leader named Pancho Villa had tried to take over the government. At first the United States believed that Villa was fighting for the political rights of the Mexican people and supported his actions. But when stories of Villa's brutality reached Wilson, the president changed his mind and sent the U.S. Army to stop the rebellion. The change in U.S. policy enraged Villa, and his men began murdering U.S. citizens wherever they found them. The two armies chased one another back and forth across the border.

This particular night, Will had planned to comment on the troubles the U.S. Army was having. In spite of his popularity, Will considered himself nothing more than an ordinary cowboy who had learned to spin a rope a little and who had learned to read the daily papers a little. Now he was expected to go out on the stage and tease the president of the United States. Will later said, "Well, I am not kidding you when I tell you that I was scared to death."

Stage hands had to push the comedian out on the stage. Will slowly made a loop and began twirling his rope. The first thing he said was, "I am kinder nervous here tonight." This remark was so obviously true that it charmed the audience. Will then made a few comments about a former presidential candidate, and President Wilson laughed. The president's reaction gave Will the courage to start talking about the trouble in Mexico.

"A comedian can only last till he either takes himself serious or his audience takes him serious, and I don't want either one of those to happen to me till I'm dead (if then)."

51

Watching the president anxiously out of the corner of his eye, Will said, "I see where they have captured Villa. Yep, they got him in the morning papers, and the afternoon ones let him get away." Again the president laughed. Will relaxed a bit and joked about the U.S. Army's lack of preparation for war, saying that it would have to borrow a gun if it ever wanted to fight a battle. Then Will said that the soldiers chased Villa into Mexico but were forced to retreat when they ran into a lot of government red tape. Each time Will made a remark, he watched to see the president's reaction.

President Wilson enjoyed Will's act immensely and laughed hardest at the jokes about himself. Wilson even repeated one of the jokes in a speech he gave in Boston. Will said later that his performance for Wilson was the "proudest and most successful night" of his stage career.

Will performed for and then came to know many important world figures, and he even counted some of them among his friends. Cowboys or princes, laborers or millionaires, Will treated them all in the same friendly, open manner. He could talk to anyone because he was everyone's friend. Will accomplished many amazing things in his life, but he is probably best remembered for saying "I never met a man I didn't like."

He soon gained a reputation for kindness and generosity that was unusual among show-business people. His fellow entertainers admired his common sense and often sought his advice. An out-of-work actor could always count on Will to help him over a rough spot. The assistance Will gave

"No, I don't think I ever hurt any man's feelings by my little gags. I know I never willfully did it. When I have to do that to make a living, I will quit."

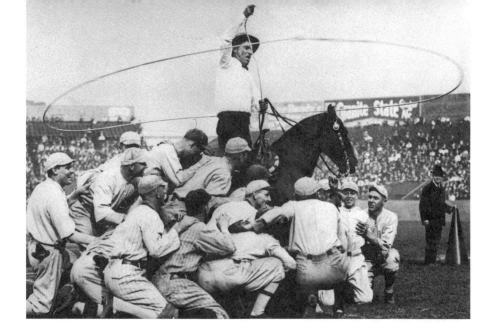

Fred Stone is a good example of the cowboy's unselfish nature. Fred, a young musical-comedy actor, was starring in a new show at the Knickerbocker Theater in New York and needed to learn some rope tricks. He hired someone from Oklahoma to teach him, but, before Fred could learn the tricks, the fellow went home.

When Will heard about the young star's predicament, he offered his services. Fred was delighted to have the opportunity to learn from a master like Will. He quickly picked up the rope-spinning tricks he needed for his act and regularly used them as part of his routine. Will's kindness launched a friendship that lasted many years. It never occurred to Will that he might hurt his own chances by sharing his roping know-how with another performer. Will's unfailing generosity earned him the love and respect of those around him all his life.

Making a giant loop, Will ropes a baseball team. A big fan, Will always kept up on the latest scores and winning plays.

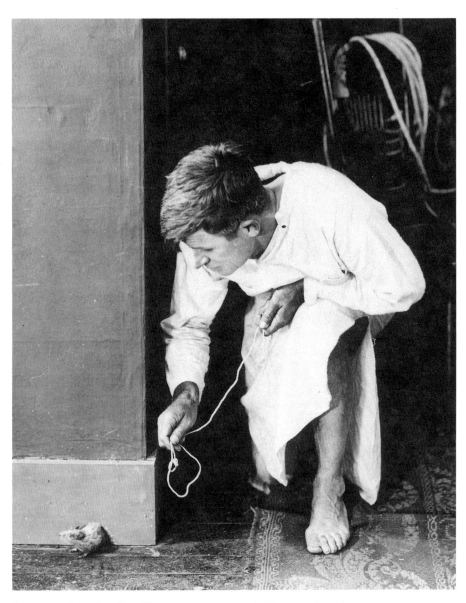

In a scene from the silent film The Ropin' Fool, *Will attempts to lasso a mouse.*

6 A Hollywood Career

After Will had mustered the courage to talk to an audience while spinning his rope, he became a show-business sensation. In 1919 he accepted an offer from film producer Samuel Goldwyn to appear in movies. Will went to Hollywood, California, and learned to be an actor. At this time, the film industry had not yet discovered how to make movies with sound. So Will had to rely on his appearance and actions to tell the story. He enjoyed making films and once remarked, "It's the only business where you can sit out front and applaud yourself."

Some of the pictures Will starred in were "Westerns," movies that featured life in the western United States in the 1800s. On a movie lot one day, a director was telling Will about a scene that required him to ride a horse. The director said that a stunt man made up to look like Will would do the riding. Having someone else ride for him did not sit very well with Will, but he didn't argue. Certain that actions would speak

"An actor is a fellow that just has a little more monkey in him than the fellow that can't act."

louder than words, he looked around and saw a stagehand leading a saddled mare. Will took the reins in his hand, leaped into the saddle, and galloped across the lot cowboy style. The director instantly realized that Will Rogers was not a "Broadway cowboy."

Another time Will was doing a scene that required him to mount a horse in a corral and ride him to a creek, where the horse would toss him off its back. Each time Will tried the scene, the half-trained horse threw him before he got out of the corral. Will finally became exasperated. When the director complained about Will's problems with the scenes, Will offered this suggestion: "Listen, if you want me to do this scene, you get a corral that's nearer the creek. Or better still, find some creek that's nearer a corral."

Will liked the warm climate of southern California so much that he decided to make the state his permanent home. He moved Betty, the kids, and all the family's dogs and horses from New York to Hollywood, where Will had bought a house. Soon after the move, the three boys came down with a serious illness called diphtheria. Will was working on a movie near San Francisco in northern California, and immediately set out for home when he heard the news. But by the time he reached Hollywood, twenty-three-month-old Freddie had already died. This tragedy made it difficult for the family to stay in the Hollywood house, which was filled with memories of the toddler. The Rogers moved to nearby Beverly Hills, where they lived for almost ten years.

Will spent three years working in Hollywood, making movies such as *Jubilo, The Strange Boarder,*

"The average life of the movie is till it reaches the critic."

At the Rogers's home in Beverly Hills, Betty and Mary pose for the camera, while Will watches Bill and Jimmy play with an erector set, a construction toy made of metal.

and *Cupid the Cowpuncher.* When his contract to appear in Goldwyn's movies ran out, Will returned to the New York stage, sadly leaving his family behind. But he told his friends in New York that it was good to be back where he could use his brain instead of loafing around a movie lot. "You know," he said, "you've got to exercise your brain just like your muscles."

One night after a performance in New York, Will met with the owner of the McNaught newspaper syndicate. The owner had realized that Will's humorous comments on political happenings would make choice newspaper copy. When the newspaper representative suggested that Will write a regular column, Will said that he didn't know anything about writing, but he'd try.

Will's articles were an instant success. He wrote just as he talked—in the homey speech of a prairie cowhand. Critics were soon referring to Will Rogers as a humorist and philosopher. At

The cameras roll as Will saddles up for a scene in the 1919 film **Jubilo.**

With a typewriter perched on his lap, Will pecks out his weekly column during a break on a movie set.

first just once a week and later every day, Will pecked out "a piece for the papers" on his typewriter. His column appeared in newspapers across the country, and he became one of the highest paid writers in the newspaper business.

Shortly after Will started writing newspaper articles, he began a series of lecture tours across the United States. He visited many small cities, giving his shrewd, witty talks to people who had never seen him in person. He was able to reach the people he considered the heart and backbone of the country—the small rancher and farmer, the unskilled laborer and miner. Will said that these people had more savvy than any well-dressed theater audience. When he took his act to Sing Sing, a prison in New York, the inmates applauded his jokes so heartily that Will began to wonder if maybe the wrong people were being locked up.

Betty often accompanied Will on his lecture tours.

Will jokes with the ship's captain during a voyage to Europe. Will toured the continent as an unofficial ambassador of the United States and wrote newspaper articles that described his travels and expressed his political opinions.

7 Ambassador of Goodwill

In 1926 the *Saturday Evening Post,* a popular national magazine, persuaded Will to take a tour of Europe. The Oklahoma cowboy found himself an honored guest wherever he traveled. He interviewed kings and dictators and attended formal banquets in Britain, Italy, Spain, and other European countries. He became friends with many of the world's most powerful political leaders. They enjoyed Will's shrewd observations about the events in their own countries as well as in the United States.

Will furnished articles to the *Post,* relating his experiences as an unofficial ambassador for U.S. president Calvin Coolidge. The articles, called "Letters of a Self-Made Diplomat to his President," were read everywhere the *Post* was sold. His reports showed that he had a good understanding of world affairs. Will worried when he discovered that many of the foreign countries he visited didn't like or respect the United States. He reported to President Coolidge, "We don't

"No nation has a monopoly on good things. Each one has something that the others could well afford to adopt."

"There ain't anything that you can find in one country that you don't find is being done just about as bad in your own."

stand like a horse thief abroad....Whoever told you we did was flattering us. We don't stand as good as a horse thief."

World War I (1914–1918), a conflict that had pitted European nations against one another, had been over for eight years when Will was on the newspaper tour. He had hoped to find the old combatants once again on peaceful terms, but he discovered that their relations were far from friendly. He wrote a colorful description of some of Europe's troubles. "France and England think as much of each other as two rival gangs of Chicago gangsters. . . . Russia hates everybody so bad it would take her a week to pick out the country she hates most." Will told the president that what Russia needed was more of a sense of humor and less of a sense of revenge.

Back home people read about Will's trip and felt as if they were traveling with him. Their reaction stemmed partly from the view that Will was one of them, the personal ambassador of the working people of the United States. He even scorned fancy clothing, dressing in the comfortable clothes and battered hat that were as much a part of him as his ungrammatical speech. Will wore his old blue suit and a friendly smile to formal dinners with foreign dignitaries. He represented the heart of his country in a unique way.

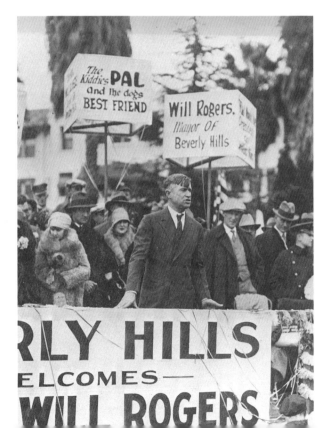

(Facing page) *In Warsaw, Poland, Will chats with a carriage driver.* (Left) *When he returned from Europe, Will was made an honorary mayor of Beverly Hills.*

8 "Can't Help Being Funny"

As much as Will loved visiting strange places and meeting new people, he liked being at home best. In the early 1920s, Will had bought property in Santa Monica, California, for a ranch, and eventually he built a home on the land. In spite of his busy schedule, he spent many happy hours at the ranch with Betty and his three remaining children. The family's favorite activity was riding, and the ranch gave them plenty of room.

The quiet, relaxed atmosphere of the ranch also gave Will the opportunity to read and to think about his newspaper articles. He often showed his articles to Betty before he sent them to be published. If she didn't understand something, he would change it. Will depended on Betty's good judgment and rarely made an important decision on any matter without talking to her first.

Once, in an interview, Betty was asked if Will was as funny at home as he was in public. "Of course he is!" she replied. "Will can't help being

"The best way to judge just how good a man is, is to find out how he stands around his home and among his kind of people."

With Jock, the family dog, at their feet, members of the Rogers family pose at their Santa Monica ranch. When this photo was taken, Jimmy (from left) was thirteen years old, Bill was seventeen, and Mary was fifteen.

funny wherever he is. His humor isn't the artificial kind that you can put on and take off like a coat. He doesn't try to be funny. He just is."

Even at home, Will never tired of practicing his rope tricks, and he took special pleasure in teaching them to his children. He also played polo, a pastime that allowed him to spend many

On the ranch, the family's horses lived in a large stable (right). The living room of the ranch house featured a rustic, western decor (below).

hours in the saddle. He formed a team with his wife and children and became an expert polo player. Will loved the competition and the thrill of riding a fast horse while trying to hit a small wooden ball with a mallet.

When he wasn't spending time with his family, Will was often traveling around the United States. On one of his cross-country lecture tours, Will developed a pain in his middle that he described as a bellyache. He was rarely sick and was proud of his good health. He had appeared almost daily on the stage for twenty years without ever missing a performance. In 1927, however,

Jimmy, Mary, Bill, and Will prepare for a polo match. Will enjoyed polo so much that he leveled a patch of his land for use as a polo field.

Will returned to California a sick man. His description of the events that followed shows how he could find humor in any situation.

"We were primitive people when I was a kid. There were only a mighty few known diseases. Gunshot wounds, broken legs, toothache, fits, and anything that hurt you from the lower end of your neck down was known as a bellyache. . . .

"Well, the bellyache hadn't shown up in years, until one spring on my tour of national annoyances. . . . When I got home they called in a doctor. He gave me some powders. The pain just thrived on those powders. I never saw a pain pick up so quick as it did when the powders hit it. . . . Finally, my wife called in Dr. White, a famous physician.

'What part of your stomach hurts?' he asked.

"Practically all of it, Doc. . . .

"'. . . It's the gallbladder—just what I was afraid of.' Now you all know what that word 'afraid of,'

The family pets—including horses and cows—made themselves at home on the ranch. Here, the family watches as Jimmy wrestles with a calf named Sarah.

Although Will developed many hobbies throughout his lifetime, one of his favorite activities was still roping cattle.

when spoken by a doctor leads to. . . . He then says, 'We operate.'

"My wife says, 'Operate?'

"And as soon as I came to enough I says, 'Operate?'

"Well, the household was up bright and early the next morning to get old Dad off to the hospital. The whole place was what the novelist would call agog. Even the chauffeur—part-time—had the old car shined up. This going to the hospital was a new thing to me. . . . I had never been sick a day in my life. . . .

"There was a kind of a little balcony up above the operating room floor where people with a well-developed sense of humor could sit and see other people cut up. It must be loads of fun. But there wasn't a soul in there for my operation. I felt kind of disappointed. I thought, 'Well, here I am, maybe playing my last act, and it is to an empty house. . . .'

"Next thing I knew I heard the nurse on one side and my wife on the other saying, 'Lay perfectly still, you're all right. You are fine now. Just relax.'

"Finally this ether got to leaving me and I sort of remembered what the operation had been for. I asked them, 'Did you get any gallstones?' Yes, they had got some. A couple of sizable dimensions, but nothing in any way approaching what could be used for exhibition purposes. I felt right then that the operation had been a failure. . . . "

"Personally, I have always felt that the best doctor in the world is the veterinarian. He can't ask his patients what is the matter—he's got to just know."

In this cartoon dating from his 1927 hospital stay, Will holds a map that leads the way to his gallbladder.

Will pages through the newspaper during a break in the shooting of the talking film Down to Earth.

9 Movies and Radio

In 1929 Will received another offer to work in Hollywood, where films were now being made with sound. William Fox, the head of Fox Studios, persuaded Will to try his hand with the "talkies."

Will was an immediate success. He made twenty-one feature films at Fox Studios, including *A Connecticut Yankee, Young as You Feel, State Fair,* and *Handy Andy.* With sound in the film, Will had a chance to show his real ability. He gave fine performances as a happy-go-lucky tramp, a country doctor, a hog-raising farmer, a banker, and a horse trader. Will had an extraordinary ability to make people forget that he was a comedian. The sincerity with which he played his various roles was remarkably convincing.

Will never lost his easygoing manner in the artificial, make-believe world of Hollywood. Although he became the highest paid movie star of his time, he always kept his simplicity and genuine friendliness. He wandered around the movie set in overalls, cowboy boots, and an old

" *I am proud of the fact that there is not a human being that I have got it in for. I never met a man I didn't like.* **"**

sweater, looking more like a working cowpuncher than a Hollywood star.

Instead of using the luxurious dressing room that the studio provided for him, Will preferred living out of his big car, where he kept a change of clothes and his typewriter. When Will was not needed in front of the camera, he would pull out his typewriter and sit on the running board along the side of the car. Balancing the machine on his knees, he would tap out his piece for the papers.

In the 1933 hit State Fair *(above),* Will tends to Blue Boy, *a prize-winning hog. After filming the movie, Will helped find a new home for his costar in a California agricultural school (right).*

Although the movie studio provided Will with a dressing room, he liked to write his newspaper column from his car.

Will had one more outlet for his boundless energy and talent. Radio was fast becoming the chief source of news and entertainment in the United States. Almost every living room proudly displayed one of the heavy wooden radio cabinets that were the style of the day. The radio brought Will's soft Oklahoma drawl into homes throughout the country.

Surrounded by a small audience, Will (center left) *makes a radio broadcast in Pittsburgh, Pennsylvania. Over the years, Will's homey radio voice crackled through the airwaves to households all across the United States.*

Will felt just as comfortable chatting with famous people, such as First Lady Eleanor Roosevelt (right), as he did with ordinary U.S. citizens. During the hard times of the Great Depression in the 1930s, Will greeted schoolchildren at a soup kitchen in Arkansas (facing page).

He charmed the public in his radio programs, during his lecture tours, and through his newspaper articles by being himself at all times. He gave his honest opinion of the nation's politics, its public organizations, and its social habits. He ridiculed what was false and pompous and showed ordinary people that their leaders were human, with the same faults and weaknesses as anyone might have. Will talked to the people in a language they could understand, and he brightened their days with his infectious chuckle.

In 1935 Will posed with his luggage and typewriter in Alaska's Matanuska Valley.

10 The Last Trip

Early in his career, Will had learned to take advantage of air travel. This mode of transportation suited his restless nature and love of speed. But in the 1920s and 1930s, the airplane was still a new invention, and many people thought flying was dangerous and foolhardy. Will ignored them, but he did listen to Betty when she asked him not to become a pilot himself.

At every opportunity, Will praised the skill of the brave pilots who flew the daily mail routes in modified military planes. These flights—many of which took off at night—could be dangerous, and some airmail pilots died in crashes. But Will promoted flying as a sound and profitable business venture. In fact, he had a special government permit that allowed him to fly in any mail plane, and he logged more than 500,000 miles of flight during his lifetime.

The plane ride that really sold Will on flying was one he had made with Billy Mitchell, the maverick army pilot. In the 1920s, Mitchell had

“We are living in great times. A fellow can't afford to die now with all this excitement going on.”

Dressed in flight gear, Will kisses Betty good-bye before boarding a mail plane.

Will greatly admired Charles Lindbergh (left), *who flew alone across the Atlantic Ocean in 1927.*

publicly pressed the government to form an air force independent of the army and navy—a demand that had outraged his army superiors. Will was also well acquainted with Charles Lindbergh, who had made the first nonstop, solo flight across the Atlantic Ocean in 1927.

One of Will's ambitions was to become "the world's airplane reporter." He wanted to fly to the troubled areas of the world and report the news as it was happening. To get to these trouble spots, he needed a pilot of great skill, and for this Will depended on his friend Wiley Post.

Wiley was a skillful and daring aviator. He grew up in Oklahoma, where he gained a reputation for being good with machinery. Despite losing an eye in an accident in the Oklahoma oil fields, Wiley got his pilot's license.

"If you live right, death is a joke to you as far as fear is concerned."

In his plane, the *Winnie Mae,* Wiley set many world records for both speed and endurance. He also flew as a test pilot for the Lockheed Aircraft Company, and he later was a commercial pilot for two airlines. In 1934 Wiley designed a rubber flying suit that could supply oxygen and maintain constant pressure at high altitudes. His experiments in high-altitude flight provided aeronautical engineers with information that led to the development of the pressurized cabins used in modern aircraft. The *Winnie Mae* was later placed in the Smithsonian Institution alongside Lindbergh's *Spirit of St. Louis.*

In the early days of flying, pilots had to fly without the aid of instruments, and in open cockpits they were vulnerable to all kinds of weather. The early pilots often followed telephone poles, flying low enough to see the ground clearly. They sometimes made emergency landings in farm fields or in any available flat open space. The planes had no radios, and airports were very scarce.

None of these hazardous conditions daunted Will, who had long wanted to fly across the Arctic Circle—an area dubbed "the roof of the world." He and Wiley had discussed the trip often. The idea grew, and in 1935 Wiley started building the plane that would take both men on their journey. The plane was designed for long-distance travel and equipped with a powerful engine. It also had fixed landing gear that could be fitted with wheels, skis, or pontoons for water landings.

In August 1935, Wiley and Will flew from Seattle, Washington, northwestward to Alaska. On one stop, they visited the pioneers of the Matanuska Valley, near Anchorage. The U.S.

"Why is it the good ones are the ones that go? That's one thing about an ornery guy, you never hear of him dying. He is into everything else but a coffin."

Will (on airplane wing) *and Wiley Post signed many autographs during their stops in Alaska.*

Will and Wiley prepare for takeoff.

government had brought in these settlers from the Midwest to farm the valley's muddy soil and to increase Alaska's population. Will walked around the valley, talking with the hardy people who had made the wilderness their home. One man gave Will some cookies he had baked. Will thanked him and said jokingly, "If Wiley has trouble getting the plane off the ground, I'll throw these out first."

These tough pioneers were Will's last audience. The next word anyone had of Will was a tragic radio message from a lonely outpost at Point Barrow, the northernmost tip of Alaska. An Inuit who had seen the plane crash ran fifteen miles to report the news of the two dead men who were inside. He described them as a man with rag over his sore eye and a big man with boots.

The world was stunned by the loss of its beloved humorist. But Will died as he had lived—searching for new sights and new faces and enjoying each minute of the day to its fullest.

*Near Point Barrow—
the most northerly spot
in Alaska—Inuit view
the wreckage of
Wiley's plane.*

Epilogue

On August 16, 1935, radio broadcasts and newspaper headlines reported Will's death to the nation and the world. The news shocked Americans, who grieved for the man who had become a part of their everyday lives. Over the years, people had grown used to reading his weekly articles, listening to his radio shows, and watching his movies. Will's wry humor brought national and international events into focus for Americans from all walks of life.

In the years following Will's death, his family kept busy. Betty ran the ranch, handled the family's finances, and spent time with her children and friends. She also wrote articles about Will's life, which were published as a book in 1941. Betty died in 1944 at the age of sixty-five.

Bill—Will and Betty's oldest child—became a newspaper editor and publisher and was elected to Congress in 1940. Later he worked as an actor and commercial spokesperson. Mary, who died in 1990, performed on Broadway. After a brief

66What constitutes a life well spent anyway? Love and admiration from your fellow men is all that anyone can ask.99

marriage in the 1950s, she spent much of her time traveling abroad. Jim Rogers also became an actor, appearing mostly in Westerns of the 1930s and 1940s. He bought a ranch near Bakersfield, California.

In her will, Betty left the ranch in Santa Monica to the state of California, and the site became the Will Rogers State Historical Park. Visitors can see the Rogers's house just as it looked when the family lived there. Another place to learn more

"I never met a man I didn't like"

In a scene from the 1990s hit musical the Will Rogers Follies, *the cast—including the character of Will Rogers* (center)*—finishes up a song and dance number.*

about Will's life is at the Will Rogers Memorial in Claremore, Oklahoma, near Will's birthplace. The memorial, which opened in 1938, contains a museum and a library.

In 1991 a musical called the *Will Rogers Follies* opened on Broadway and later toured the country. The character of Will Rogers twirled his rope, told jokes, and introduced lavish production numbers. Toward the end of the show, the actor playing Will gave a speech about unemployment that Will originally delivered in 1931.

Although much of Will's humor was tied to his times, his good-natured manner and concern for the everyday citizen is timeless. Audiences watching the *Will Rogers Follies* are appreciating his wit, wisdom, and insight in the 1990s just as much as audiences had in earlier decades.

It's only the inspiration of those who die that makes those who live realize what constitutes a useful life.

Sources

p. 9   source unknown

p. 10 May 4, 1930, *Will Rogers' Weekly Articles: The Hoover Years, 1929–1931*, Steven K. Gragert, ed. Stillwater: Oklahoma State University Press, 1981.

p. 13 source unknown

p. 17 source unknown

p. 22 August 14, 1930, *Will Rogers' Daily Telegrams: The Hoover Years, 1929–1931*, James M. Smallwood, ed. Stillwater: Oklahoma State University Press, 1978

p. 24 August 31, 1924, *Will Rogers' Weekly Articles: The Harding/Coolidge Years, 1922–1925*, James M. Smallwood, ed. Stillwater: Oklahoma State University Press, 1981.

p. 27 source unknown

p. 29 "A Real American Cowboy": *Reminiscences of Rouben Mamoulian*, Columbia University Oral History Collection, New York.

p. 30 source unknown

p. 31 source unknown

p. 35 May 24, 1925, *Will Rogers' Weekly Articles: The Harding/Coolidge Years, 1922–1925*, James M. Smallwood, ed. Stillwater: Oklahoma State University Press, 1980.

p. 38 November 4, 1928, *Will Rogers' Weekly Articles: The Coolidge Years, 1927–1929*, James M. Smallwood, ed. Stillwater: Oklahoma State University Press, 1981.

p. 41 *The Tulsa Daily World*, Jan. 8, 1933, IV, p. 4

p. 45 June 1, 1930, *Will Rogers' Weekly Articles: The Hoover Years, 1929–1931*, Steven K. Gragert, ed. Stillwater: Oklahoma State University Press, 1981.

p. 46 source unknown

p. 48 January 13, 1924, *Will Rogers' Weekly Articles: The Harding/Coolidge Years, 1922–1925*, James M. Smallwood, ed. Stillwater: Oklahoma State University Press, 1980.

p. 51 June 28, 1932, *Will Rogers' Weekly Articles: The Hoover Years, 1931–1933*, Steven K. Gragert, ed. Stillwater: Oklahoma State University Press, 1982.

p. 52 *Will Rogers' Weekly Articles: The Harding/Coolidge Years, 1922–1925*, James M. Smallwood, ed. Stillwater: Oklahoma State University Press, 1980.

p. 55 November 4, 1928, *Will Rogers' Weekly Articles: The Coolidge Years, 1927–1929*, James M. Smallwood, ed. Stillwater: Oklahoma State University Press, 1981.

p. 56 source unknown

p. 60 June 4, 1929, *Will Rogers' Daily Telegrams: The Coolidge Years, 1926–1929*, James M. Smallwood, ed. Stillwater: Oklahoma State University Press, 1978.

p. 63 November 30, 1930, *Will Rogers' Weekly Articles: The Hoover Years, 1929–1931*, Steven K. Gragert, ed. Stillwater: Oklahoma State University Press, 1981.

p. 64 source unknown

p. 67 source unknown

p. 73 source unknown

p. 75 January 8, 1933, *Will Rogers' Weekly Articles: The Hoover Years, 1931–1933*, Steven K. Gragert, ed. Stillwater: Oklahoma State University Press, 1982.

p. 83 May 24, 1925, *Will Rogers' Weekly Articles: The Harding/Coolidge Years, 1922–1925*, James M. Smallwood, ed. Stillwater: Oklahoma State University Press, 1980.

p. 85 Ibid.

p. 86 Ibid.

p. 91 August 9, 1925, Ibid.

p. 93 May 24, 1925, Ibid.

Index

Photo Acknowledgments

Cover photographs courtesy of the Will Rogers Memorial and Birthplace, Claremore, Oklahoma

All photos courtesy of the Will Rogers Memorial and Birthplace, Claremore, Oklahoma, except the following: Kansas State Historical Society, Topeka, Kansas, pp. 18, 19 (top); Wyoming State Museum, p. 19 (bottom); Museum of Modern Art/Film Stills Archive, pp. 26, 59, 76; Library of Congress, p. 28; Ford Album Collection (77.1314), Photographic Archives, University of Louisville, p. 36; Culver Pictures, Inc., pp. 49 (bottom), 58, 60, 74; AP/Wide World Photos, p. 89; courtesy of Phil Simmons, p. 93